Date: 5/24/12

ABDO
Publishing Company

NERVOUS
System

BODY SYSTEMS

A Buddy Book by **Sarah Tieck**

Buddy BOOKS
Body Systems

VISIT US AT
www.abdopublishing.com

Published by ABDO Publishing Company, 8000 West 78th Street, Edina, Minnesota 55439.

Printed in the United States of America, North Mankato, Minnesota.
092010
012011
 PRINTED ON RECYCLED PAPER

Coordinating Series Editor: Rochelle Baltzer
Contributing Editors: Megan M. Gunderson, BreAnn Rumsch, Marcia Zappa
Graphic Design: Jenny Christensen
Cover Photograph: *iStockphoto:* ©iStockphoto.com/mocker_bat.
Interior Photographs/Illustrations: *Eighth Street Studio* (pp. 5, 22); *iStockphoto:* ©iStockphoto.com/blwilliamsphoto (p. 19), ©iStockphoto.com/carlofranco (p. 30), ©iStockphoto.com/EMPPhotography (p. 22), ©iStockphoto.com/lenorlux (p. 27), ©iStockphoto.com/LindaYolanda (p. 23), ©iStockphoto.com/markgoddard (p. 21), ©iStockphoto.com/RapidEye (p. 9), ©iStockphoto.com/VMJones (p. 21); *Peter Arnold, Inc.*: MedicalRF/The Medical File (p. 7), Medicimage/The Medical File (p. 27); *Photo Researchers, Inc.*: BSIP (p. 15), Laguna Design (p. 17); *Shutterstock*: goldenangel (p. 29), JinYoung Lee (p. 11), Daniel Korzeniewski (p. 25), jan kranendonk (p. 11), Micha? Pucha?a (p. 30), zimmytws (p. 13).

Library of Congress Cataloging-in-Publication Data

Tieck, Sarah, 1976-
  Nervous system / Sarah Tieck.
    p. cm. -- (Body systems)
  ISBN 978-1-61613-500-3
  1. Nervous system--Juvenile literature. I. Title.
  QP361.5.T54 2011
  612.8--dc22
                                2010019654

Table of Contents

Amazing Body

Your body is amazing! It does thousands of things each day. You can jump, hear, and touch because your body parts work together.

Groups of body parts make up body systems. Each system does important work. The nervous system controls your senses, movements, and basic body functions. Let's learn more about it!

Your nervous system's central parts are in your head and back. But, this system has connections all over your body.

Working Together

Your brain and spinal cord make up your central nervous system (CNS). Nerves that connect them to the rest of your body make up your outer nervous system. Together, they send messages between your body parts.

Your brain's messages travel through nerves. When they reach body parts they can cause actions. Other times, nerves send messages to the brain. Then, your brain decides how to use the information.

YOUR NERVOUS SYSTEM

Brain

Nerve

Spinal Cord

All in Your Head

The control center of the nervous system is the brain. It is in your head. A thin layer of cells and a bony case called a skull **protect** your brain.

The brain looks like a gooey lump. But, it is very powerful. Its main parts are the brain stem, the cerebellum, and the cerebrum.

 How It Sounds

cerebellum (sehr-uh-BEH-luhm)
cerebrum (suh-REE-bruhm)

YOUR BRAIN

Cerebrum

Cerebellum

Brain Stem

The brain stem passes messages from the brain to the body. It also controls body functions, such as breathing and your heartbeat.

The cerebellum is a small part of your brain. It controls balance and helps muscles move together.

The cerebrum is the center of thinking. It has two halves. Each side supports different types of thinking. The cerebrum also controls speech, feelings, memories, and some movements.

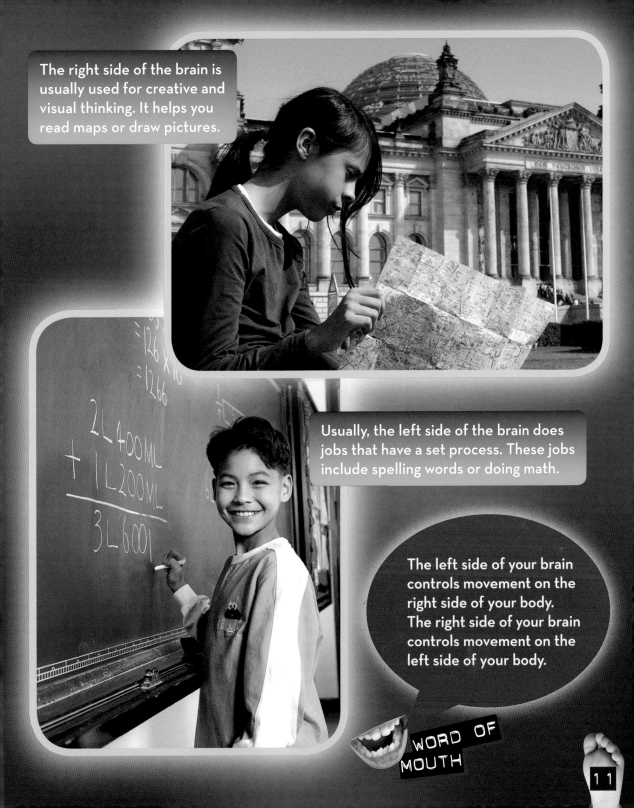

The right side of the brain is usually used for creative and visual thinking. It helps you read maps or draw pictures.

Usually, the left side of the brain does jobs that have a set process. These jobs include spelling words or doing math.

The left side of your brain controls movement on the right side of your body. The right side of your brain controls movement on the left side of your body.

WORD OF MOUTH

The Spinal Cord

Your spinal cord is along the center of your back and neck. It is a long group of nerves. Your spine surrounds the nerves to **protect** them.

Messages move back and forth through the spinal cord. Some travel from the brain to other parts of the body. Others start in the body and go to the brain.

WORD OF MOUTH

Your spinal cord is light. It weighs just over one ounce (28 g).

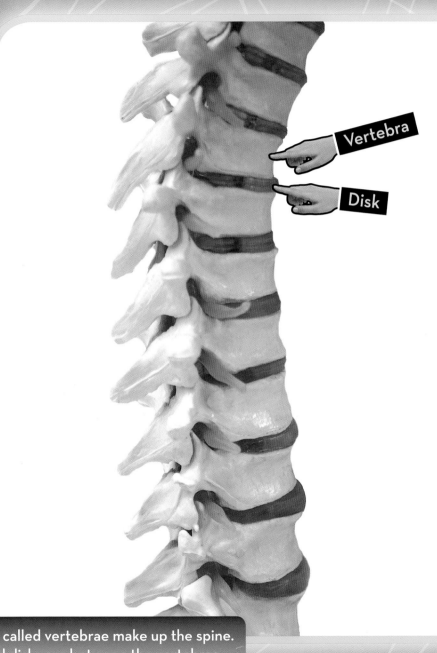

Vertebra

Disk

Bones called vertebrae make up the spine. Special disks are between the vertebrae. They cushion the spine and help it bend.

Oh, the Nerve!

Your nervous system is made up of thousands of cells called neurons. Neurons quickly pass messages along nerves.

A message goes from one neuron toward another neuron. Armlike parts called axons and dendrites help move the message.

Between neurons, the message crosses over a space called a synapse. Special chemicals carry the message across the space.

How It Sounds

neuron (NOO-rahn)
axon (AK-sahn)
dendrite (DEHN-drite)
synapse (SIH-naps)

YOUR NEURONS

Neuron Cell Body

Dendrite

Axon

Synapse

Dendrite

Neuron Cell Body

Axon

15

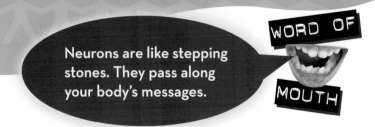

There are different types of neurons. These include interneurons, motor neurons, and sensory neurons. Most interneurons are in your CNS. Motor and sensory neurons are found throughout your body.

Motor neurons bring your brain's messages to your muscles, causing actions. Sensory neurons get messages from your senses and organs and bring them to your brain. Interneurons connect your motor and sensory neurons.

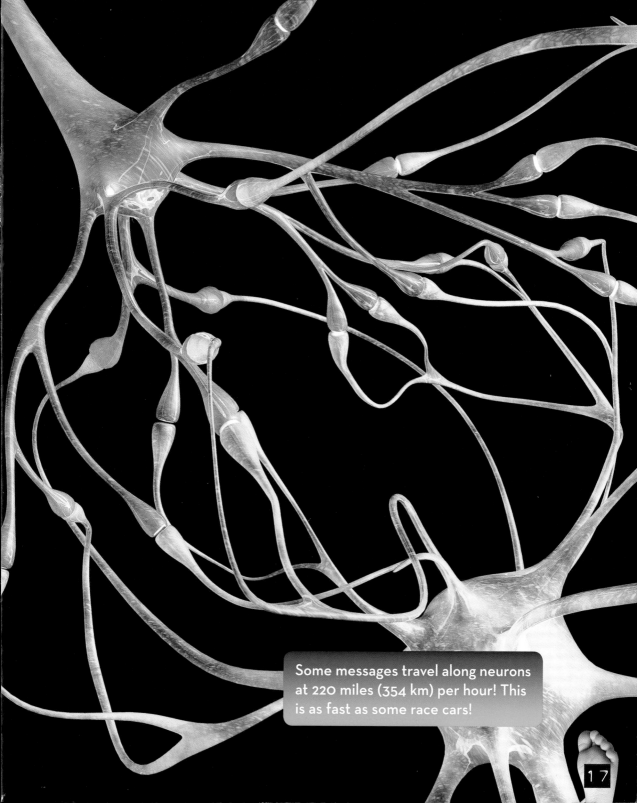

Some messages travel along neurons at 220 miles (354 km) per hour! This is as fast as some race cars!

The Senses

Sensory neurons tell your brain about the world around you. They allow you to taste, touch, hear, smell, and see.

Imagine eating ice cream. Cells called receptors gather information about your treat. Sensory neurons carry these messages to your brain. You recognize the ice cream as sweet and cold. You probably know the flavor, too!

Certain areas of your body are more sensitive to touch than others. These include the tips of your tongue, nose, and fingers.

WORD OF MOUTH

Your tongue has taste buds. These receive messages about food.

Reflexes

Your body has reflex actions. They happen without you even thinking about them! For example, if you touch a hot stove, you quickly move your hand.

Your body sends messages through sensory neurons when it notices changes. Motor neurons get the messages. They tell your muscles to act fast!

Sighing, breathing, and blinking are all reflexes.

WORD OF MOUTH

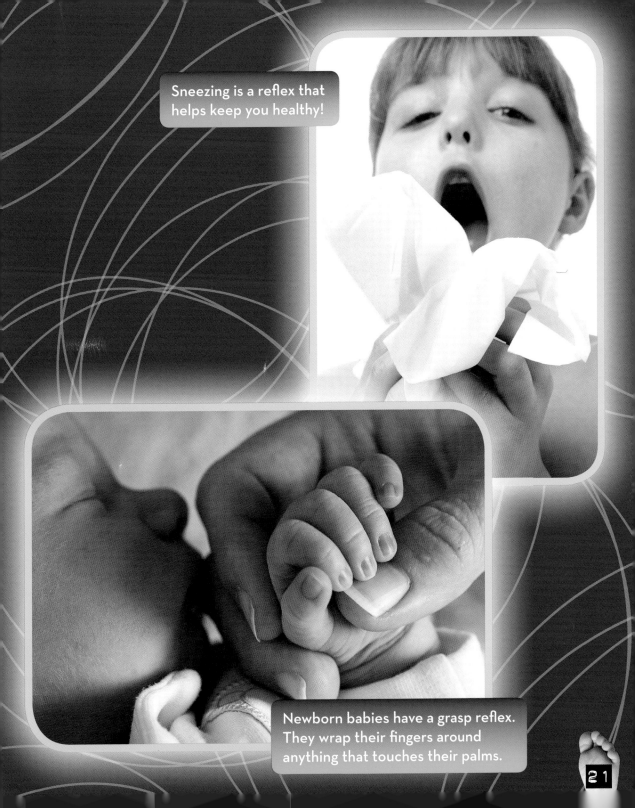

Sneezing is a reflex that helps keep you healthy!

Newborn babies have a grasp reflex. They wrap their fingers around anything that touches their palms.

Brain Food

Does your nervous system ever get a break?

No! Your nervous system is at work even while you sleep. It makes sure you breathe, turn, and dream. It may let out chemicals that tell your body to grow. And if there is danger, it wakes you up.

How do you taste different foods?

People have taste receptors called taste buds. But, they can only recognize a few basic flavors. Smell receptors in your nose work with taste buds to create thousands of flavors!

How many nerves are in your outer nervous system?

There are 24 large nerves that run between your brain and your body. There are 62 nerves that run from your spinal cord to your body.

If your leg "falls asleep," there is pressure on the nerve. When the pressure is gone, you might feel "pins and needles."

Danger! Danger!

Your nervous system watches out for your body. It tracks when you feel heat, cold, and pain. These things may mean your body is in danger.

Your nervous system helps you act quickly. When you feel scared, your heartbeat and breathing speed up. This is often called the "fight or flight response."

If a person's nerves become blocked, messages can't get through. A doctor's visit may be necessary.

Doctors have special tools to look at a person's brain. They can also see if the spinal cord is healthy. For serious problems, doctors can offer medicine or do surgery.

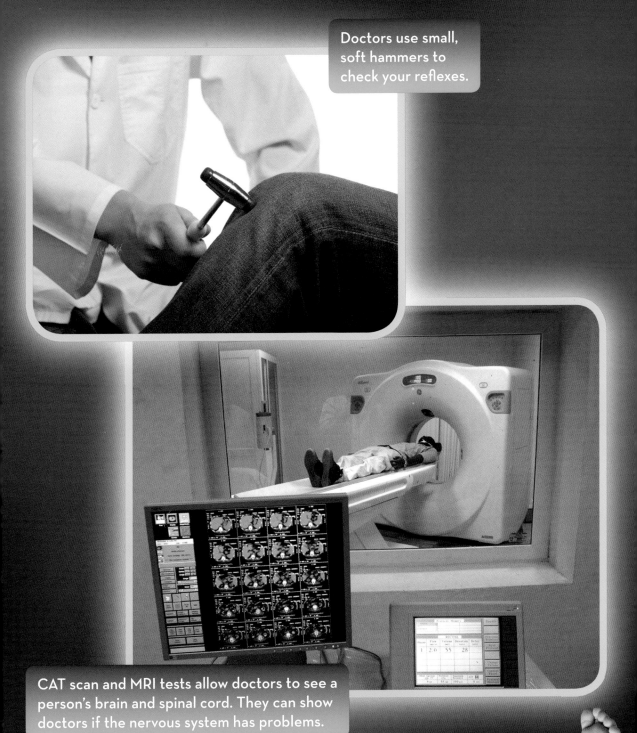

Doctors use small, soft hammers to check your reflexes.

CAT scan and MRI tests allow doctors to see a person's brain and spinal cord. They can show doctors if the nervous system has problems.

An Important System

Think of how much your nervous system does! It allows your brain and body to send messages back and forth. It often does this without you even thinking about it.

You can help **protect** your nervous system by learning about it. Then, you can make good choices to keep your body healthy.

28

Your nervous system
helps your body balance.

HEALTHY BODY FILES

BODY CARE

✔ Drink plenty of water! This helps your body make a special liquid to protect your spinal cord and brain.

✔ Even though shots are not fun, doctors give them to keep you healthy. Some shots protect your nervous system from illnesses.

CRASH TEST

✔ Wear a seat belt when riding in a car. This helps keep your brain and spinal cord safe in case of accidents.

A SAFE BRAIN

✔ Chemical fumes can harm your brain. So, don't sniff them.

✔ Remember to wear a helmet when riding a bicycle. This reduces brain injuries by about 80 percent.

Important Words

chemical (KEH-mih-kuhl) a substance that can cause reactions and changes.

function a specific job or action.

information (ihn-fuhr-MAY-shuhn) knowledge about a situation.

medicine (MEH-duh-suhn) an item used in or on the body to treat an illness, ease pain, or heal a wound.

muscles (MUH-suhls) body tissues, or layers of cells, that help move the body.

organ a body part that does a special job. The heart and the lungs are organs.

protect (pruh-TEHKT) to guard against harm or danger.

surgery (SUHRJ-ree) the treating of sickness or injury by cutting into and repairing body parts.

Web Sites

To learn more about the nervous system, visit ABDO Publishing Company online. Web sites about the nervous system are featured on our Book Links page. These links are routinely monitored and updated to provide the most current information available.

www.abdopublishing.com

Index